Presidential Trivia 2.0

Presidential Trivia 2.0

By Timothy D. Holder

Copyright 2016 by TDH Communications

Knoxville TN

Cover Design by Light House Studio

Acknowledgements

I would like to thank my wife, Angela, for being wonderful and for suggesting that I do a small book like this one.

I also appreciate my mother, Judy, for helping with the editing of several books and being a great encourager. I am grateful to my father, Charles, and my in-laws, Jack and Carol Easterday, for their love and support.

Steve Ellis, the president of Light House Studio, is a terrific Website designer and photographer. His cover art is great, too. The thing I like best about him is that he's my friend.

Presidential Trivia

1. Presidents have been inaugurated in three cities, New York City, Philadelphia, and Washington, DC.

2. Two presidents have been impeached, Andrew Johnson and Bill Clinton. Being impeached means they went on trial in the Senate. There is a difference between being impeached and being thrown out of office. Richard Nixon would have been impeached, but he resigned first.

3. Men from five different political parties have been elected president. In order of service, the parties were Federalist, Democratic-Republican, Democrat, Whig, and Republican.

4. Three presidents have died on July 4—John Adams, Thomas Jefferson, and James Monroe.

5. Donald Trump is America's 45th President even though there have only been 44 people who have occupied that position. The discrepancy is due to Grover Cleveland, who was elected twice but not in consecutive terms. He was the 22nd and 24th President.

6. Only four of the presidents have claimed no church membership—Zachary Taylor, Abraham Lincoln, Andrew Johnson, and Donald Trump—but even they indicated a belief in God.

7. During two years, 1841 and 1881, the US had 3 presidents. Both times, the president at the start of the year was replaced on Inauguration Day then the new president died soon after. In 1841 the presidents were Van Buren, Harrison, and Tyler. In the USA had Hayes, Garfield, and Arthur.

8. The four presidents carved into Mount Rushmore are George Washington, Thomas Jefferson, Abraham Lincoln, and Theodore Roosevelt.

#1 George Washington

Political Party: None

Religious Affiliation: Episcopalian

Home State when Elected: Virginia

Time of Service: 4/30/1789-3/4/1797

Birth Date: February 22, 1732

Deceased: December 14, 1799

Presidential Trivia 2.0

George Washington

1. Washington was the first of many presidents who did not have a middle name.

2. In public, he only prayed while standing up, even if those around him were seated or kneeling.

3. Washington never chopped down a cherry tree as a child, nor did he confess to his father, saying, "I cannot tell a lie." The story was invented by a biographer who thought school kids needed a role model. In other words, the biographer told a lie because he wanted to encourage kids not to lie. How's that for irony?

4. Here's some more irony for you: Though he is called "the Father of our Country," Washington never had biological children of his own. He helped raise Martha's kids from her first marriage (her first husband was deceased), but that was it.

5. Washington is sometimes listed as a Federalist, but he never joined that or any other political party. In fact, he hated political parties because he thought they were divisive. The reason some call him a Federalist is

because he increasingly favored Federalist policies over the course of his time in office. Nevertheless, he would have felt that it was an attack on his honor to link him with a political party after he publicly asserted his independence from them.

6. During John Adams' term as President, high-ranking Federalist Alexander Hamilton urged Washington to come out of retirement and serve as President again in 1800. Washington refused, which was for the best since Washington actually died before the 1800 election anyway.

7. Washington's false teeth weren't made of wood. He tried a variety of options that included ivory, bone, and other stuff.

8. In his younger days, Washington was an exceptionally strong man, physically speaking. He was emotionally tough, too, but that's not what I am talking about here.

9. For as great a man as he was, Washington was also very concerned about his image. It really upset him when newspaper commentators said unkind things about him.

10. Washington considered serving only one term as President. He was tired and relatively old. And he wanted to see the constitutional process work without his unifying presence to hold the country together. Alexander Hamilton and Thomas Jefferson, the leaders of the two political parties at that time, urged Washington to serve for another four years for the good of the country. Imagine the most popular Republican and the most popular Democrat of today both agreeing on who the best President would be. George Washington was one of a kind.

11. His wife, Martha, was quite disappointed by George's decision to serve four more years. She wanted him to retire.

12. As President, Washington never shook hands with people. He felt that as President of the United States, he should be more formal than that. He bowed instead.

#2 John Adams

Political Party: Federalist

Religious Affiliation: Unitarian

Home State when Elected: Massachusetts

Time of Service: 3/4/1797-3/4/1801

Birth Date: October 30, 1735

Deceased: July 4, 1826

John Adams

1. Here's something people don't think about: Since Washington had fake teeth, John Adams was the first president with a mouth full of real ones.

2. Adams and Thomas Jefferson died on the same day—the 50th anniversary of the signing of the Declaration of Independence, a document which both men (but mainly Jefferson) helped write.

3. Adams' last words were, "Jefferson still lives." This wasn't true, though, since Jefferson had died several hours earlier.

4. Jefferson and Adams were friends both early and late in their lives. They spent several years in between as enemies primarily due to their political differences (and Jefferson's handling of their differences).

5. Adams' Unitarian beliefs (as opposed to a belief in the Trinity) would technically make him a heretic to Christians with a more literal belief in the Bible (like me). Interestingly, Adams referred to himself as "a church-going animal."

6. Adams was the only one of the first five Presidents to not be part of the so-called Virginia Dynasty.

7. He was also the only one of the first five to be elected to just one term, then defeated in his bid for re-election. Ouch.

8. Adam's wife, Abigail, is considered to be the most brilliant of the wives of the Founding Fathers.

9. Adams served as the defense attorney for some Redcoats who were charged with manslaughter in the deaths of a few colonists during the "Boston Massacre." Adams defended the British soldiers even though he was politically ambitious and feared his role in the trial would ruin his political career.

10. As president, Adams was criticized for his alleged desire to be a king instead of just our Chief Executive. Because of this and Adams' losing battle with his waistline, some of his less sensitive critics began calling him, "His Rotundity." Ouch again.

11. Adams was the first president to live in the White House.

#3 Thomas Jefferson

Political Party: Democratic-Republican

Religious Affiliation: Deist

Home State when Elected: Virginia

Time of Service: 3/4/1801-3/4/1809

Birth Date: April 13, 1743

Deceased: July 4, 1826

Thomas Jefferson

1. He was a proponent of the Louisiana Purchase, which doubled the size of the US and officially ended Napoleon's dream of having a French Empire in North America. I'd explain why Napoleon was willing to sell Louisiana, but this isn't *French Trivia 2.0*.

2. Was Jefferson a hypocrite? He said the federal government shouldn't do anything unless the Constitution specifically said it could, but there was nothing in the Constitution about the government spending money on buying foreign land, which is what the Louisiana Territory was.

3. Was Jefferson a hypocrite (part II)? He famously wrote that "all men are created equal," yet of the 300+ slaves he owned over the course of his life, he only freed seven.

4. Jefferson was the only one of the first 4 presidents to not proclaim a national day of Thanksgiving.

5. He was the first president to have also been a governor. He served in Virginia.

6. Jefferson was also the first president to serve his entire tenure in one national capital. He started and finished in Washington DC.

7. Jefferson was the first president to have two VPs. First there was Aaron Burr, but he had some issues (Burr has been accused of trying to steal the presidency from Jefferson, murdering Alexander Hamilton in a duel, and committing treason against the United States of America, but nobody's perfect). George Clinton was on the ticket for Jefferson's second term.

8. Would Jefferson be more comfortable as a Republican or a Democrat today? Jefferson shrunk the size and strength of the federal government, but he also downsized the military and was hostile to industry.

9. Like John Adams, he died on the fiftieth anniversary of the signing of the Declaration of Independence.

10. Jefferson has been accused of having several children with a slave named Sally Hemings. There actually is a genetic link between the descendants of Jefferson and Hemings.

11. Jefferson was the first secretary of state, and he started an interesting trend (at least it was interesting to me): The third through sixth presidents had all served as secretary of state at some point before becoming president.

12. Jefferson and James Madison were the first leaders of the Democratic-Republicans, but Jefferson tried at first to lead from behind the scenes.

13. Jefferson wanted the Native Americans to adopt the moral teachings of the Bible, but he didn't want them to learn about the miracles written in it. Jefferson didn't believe in miracles, and thought they would needlessly confuse the Native Americans. This prompted Jefferson to have a version of the Bible published without the miracle stories. I find this very disturbing.

Presidential Trivia 2.0

#4 James Madison

Political Party: Democratic-Republican

Religious Affiliation: Episcopalian

Home State when Elected: Virginia

Time of Service: 3/4/1809-3/4/1817

Birth Date: March 16, 1751

Deceased: June 28, 1836

18

James Madison

1. Madison was about 5'5" tall, and he weighed about 100 pounds as President.

2. It was during the Madison administration that people began calling the executive mansion the "White House."

3. Madison briefly considered a career in the ministry as a young man. One of the main reasons he decided against it was he lacked confidence in his speaking voice. This would have been a bigger issue back then given their lack of public address systems in Madison's day.

4. Jefferson called him, "The greatest man in America." That's nice, especially coming from Jefferson who was so popular in the country (even if he isn't so popular with me).

5. Madison is known as the Father of the Constitution for the role he played in the writing of it.

6. He was the only president to help write *The Federalist Papers*, which extolled the virtues of the Constitution

when it was being debated for ratification by the states. The other two writers were Alexander Hamilton and John Jay.

7. He was offered the position of secretary of state under Washington after Jefferson had resigned. Madison declined.

8. Madison was the first of only two presidents to use a VP who had already been the vice president for somebody else. Madison's first VP was George Clinton.

9. Madison's second vice president was Elbridge Gerry. Both of Madison's vice presidents died in office.

10. Madison was the first American to be president during a war (The War of 1812).

11. When Congress wanted to commit federal dollars to the building of a road, Madison vetoed it. He liked the idea of having the road, but there is nothing in the Constitution that says the federal government has the authority to spend money that way. What would Madison think of how Congress spends money today?

#5 James Monroe

Political Party: Democratic-Republican

Religious Affiliation: Episcopalian

Home State when Elected: Virginia

Time of Service: 3/4/1817-3/4/1825

Birth Date: April 28, 1758

Deceased: July 4, 1831

James Monroe

1. Monroe fought and was wounded in the American Revolution, making him the first war hero to be president since George Washington.

2. He, Madison, and Jefferson are closely linked politically, historically, and geographically. Jefferson and Monroe in particular had plantation houses that were just a couple of miles apart.

3. Monroe ran for a seat in the first House of Representatives, but lost to James Madison of all people.

4. Monroe strongly considered competing against Madison for the presidency after Jefferson's second term. Madison had Jefferson's support though, so Monroe quickly and wisely decided to wait his turn.

5. Monroe and Madison were able to move past their rivalry, though; Monroe later served as Madison's secretary of state and as his secretary of war.

6. Monroe was an old fashioned man and that included his taste in fashion. He was the last knickers-wearing

president, making his successor, John Quincy Adams, the first man to wear long pants at his inauguration.

7. When Monroe went for re-election as president, the Federalists did not even bother putting up a candidate against him. George Washington is the only other president to run unopposed.

8. Despite the lack of a competitor, Monroe did not win 100% of the electoral votes like George Washington. Monroe's secretary of state, John Quincy Adams, received one vote. Still, Monroe had the third most lopsided Electoral College victory in American history (since Washington was elected twice)—an impressive achievement.

9. Monroe served as governor of Virginia.

#6 John Quincy Adams

Political Party: Democratic-Republican

Religious Affiliation: Unitarian

Home State when Elected: Massachusetts

Time of Service: 3/4/1825-3/4/1829

Birth Date: July 11, 1767

Deceased: February 23, 1848

John Quincy Adams

1. Adams is one of only five presidents to win the office without getting the most popular votes. The other four were Rutherford B. Hayes, Benjamin Harrison, and George W. Bush, and Donald Trump.

2. Adams is the only one of the five who was not a Republican.

3. John Quincy Adams was the first son of a president to be president himself.

4. The sixth president was also the first one to have a middle name.

5. John Quincy Adams left the Federalists for the Democratic-Republican Party partly because he felt the Federalists had treated his father poorly and partly because Quincy Adams felt that Federalists were too focused on politics and the local economy instead of national security and growth.

6. His wife, Louisa, was the first foreign-born first lady, but she was not a foreigner. Does that sound confusing? Her dad was an American diplomat, and he

was working in England. His wife, also an American, was with him, and she gave birth to Louisa while they were there.

7. He was the first president to win office without winning a majority or a plurality of the electoral vote. Because there was no clear cut winner in the election, the House of Representatives picked the president from among the top three vote getters.

8. A plurality is where the top vote getter has less than 50% of the vote but more votes than anyone else.

9. In the highly contentious Election of 1828, Adams was accused of being a pimp by the supporters of Andrew Jackson. Seriously.

10. After being voted out as president, Adams was elected to the House of Representatives, which allowed him to continue his battles with Jackson.

11. Adams was such a prolific writer that at times his hand would cramp up. Adams taught himself to write with his weaker hand. He was an unpopular president, but you have to admire his capacity to fight through adversity.

12. Adams used to skinny dip in the Potomac River. I don't admire that at all.

#7 Andrew Jackson

Political Party: Democratic

Religious Affiliation: Presbyterian

Home State when Elected: Tennessee

Time of Service: 3/4/1829-3/4/1837

Birth Date: March 15, 1767

Deceased: June 8, 1845

Andrew Jackson

1. Jackson is one of only three men to win the popular vote for the presidency at least three times. This was a feat only surpassed by Franklin Roosevelt who won it four times (Grover Cleveland equaled Jackson's mark and was the only other man to do so).

2. Like the other two presidents from Tennessee, Jackson was actually born in North Carolina, or maybe it was South Carolina. He was born somewhere along the border, so the truth is a little iffy here.

3. Either way, he was our first president to not be from either Virginia or Massachusetts.

4. In the Election of 1828, supporters of John Quincy Adams accused Jackson of being a murderer and adulterer.

5. Jackson was a national hero because of the War of 1812, specifically as a result of his victory at the Battle of New Orleans.

6. To differentiate between his supporters and those of Adams in 1828—all initially Democratic-

Republicans—Jacksonites shortened their label to "Democrats," and Adams' people began calling themselves "National Republicans." Parenthetically, those National Republicans are not directly related to today's Republicans.

7. Another thing Jackson and Adams shared besides their political party (initially) was their vice president. John C. Calhoun was Adams' VP then Calhoun served as the vice president during Jackson's first four years.

8. When the Supreme Court issued a ruling in favor of the Cherokee Native Americans, Jackson defied the court. It was the most open abuse of the principle of separation of powers in American history. It was also one example of why Jackson's critics called him "King Andrew."

9. In addition to being known as "King Andrew," Jackson was also called "Old Hickory" in reference to his toughness.

10. Adams' supporters called Jackson's wife a bigamist, which was true (her first husband had not divorced her before she married Jackson). The story embarrassed

her so much that she fainted on the spot when she found out it went public. She died two weeks later (she had a chronically bad heart). Jackson, who was easily angered anyway, blamed his political enemies for her death.

11. Jackson's election as president signaled the end of a trend. The previous four presidents had all served as secretaries of state. Jackson's successor, Martin Van Buren was also a secretary of state then the position became pretty unimportant as a stepping stone to the presidency, as Hillary Clinton would come to realize.

#8 Martin Van Buren

Political Party: Democratic

Religious Affiliation: Dutch Reformed

Home State when Elected: New York

Time of Service: 3/4/1837-3/4/1841

Birth Date: December 5, 1782

Deceased: July 24, 1862

Presidential Trivia 2.0

Martin Van Buren

1. Van Buren was the first president to have "Hail to the Chief" played right before he was inaugurated.
2. He was almost the minister (ambassador) to England, but the Senate failed to confirm him. The deciding vote against him was cast by John Calhoun, Jackson's first VP and the nemesis of both Jackson and Van Buren.
3. Van Buren is the only other president besides Thomas Jefferson to have served as both VP and secretary of state.
4. Also like Jefferson, Van Buren entered the White House as a widower.
5. He was the first president not named "Adams" to serve only one term, which might have created a secret sense of relief for some Adams family members.
6. Probably the biggest reason for Van Buren's failure to be re-elected was the terrible economic depression that ravaged the country. Depressions and recessions have occurred periodically throughout American history.
7. Van Buren's nickname was "The Little Magician."

8. He was also called "Martin Van Ruin" because of the depression he presided over. I thought that was pretty cold.

9. In 1848 Van Buren ran for president as the candidate of the Free Soil Party.

10. English was not his primary language (and he is our only president for whom that is true). Van Buren grew up as a Dutch-speaker.

#9 William Henry Harrison

Political Party: Whig

Religious Affiliation: Episcopalian

Home State when Elected: Ohio

Time of Service: 3/4/1841-4/4/1841

Birth Date: February 9, 1773

Deceased: April 4, 1841

Presidential Trivia 2.0

William Henry Harrison

1. Though Harrison rose to fame in (what was then considered) the West, he was actually born in Virginia, making him the fifth Virginian among the first nine presidents.

2. At age 68, he was the first of only three presidents to pledge to only serve one term.

3. He's most well-known for giving the longest inaugural speech as president and serving the shortest time in office (one month).

4. Harrison is also known for being the first in the string of a bizarre coincidence. Presidents elected every twenty years from 1840-1960 all died in office. Some, like Harrison, died of natural causes; others were assassinated. Some died in their first terms, some after their re-election.

5. He is the grandfather of president #23, Benjamin Harrison.

6. Harrison was the first Whig president.

7. Harrison was a hero in the War of 1812.

8. He and his wife had ten children.

#10 John Tyler

Political Party: Whig

Religious Affiliation: Episcopalian

Home State when Sworn In: Virginia

Time of Service: 4/4/1841-3/4/1845

Birth Date: March 29, 1790

Deceased: January 18, 1862

John Tyler

1. Like many of our presidents, Tyler served as a governor earlier in life. He was a governor of Virginia.
2. He was the first president to serve as the result of a death rather than by being elected on his own merit.
3. Harrison's death wasn't the only tragedy to hit the White House during this four-year period. Tyler's wife, Letitia, died in 1842.
4. Because of the way Tyler ascended to the presidency, there was some indecision over how to refer to him. Some politicians wanted to address Tyler as "Acting President." Tyler responded by ignoring such salutations. He was the president, and he was determined to be referred to that way.
5. Tyler was the first president to be born after the Constitution was adopted, making him the first president to be born as a citizen of the United States of America.
6. He was only a Whig because he hated Andrew Jackson, not out of political philosophy. Thus, when he

assumed the presidency, his agenda was a matter of great frustration to the other Whigs in the government. Over time, every member of his Cabinet resigned.

7. Tyler was incredibly unpopular by the end of his presidency. He burned his bridges with the Democrats when he became a Whig, and I already told you what the Whigs thought of him.

8. Tyler wasn't liked in his home state of Virginia until the Civil War loomed, and Virginians saw Tyler as the wise old sage who understood Washington politics but put the interests of Virginia first.

11# James K. Polk

Political Party: Democratic

Religious Affiliation: Presbyterian/Methodist

Home State when Elected: Tennessee

Time of Service: 3/4/1845-3/4/1849

Birth Date: November 2, 1795

Deceased: June 15, 1849

James K. Polk

1. He served as a governor of Tennessee.

2. Another position he held was that of Speaker of the House in the United States Congress. He is the only President to have also served in this position.

3. As late as Polk's presidency, the federal government was still so small that it did not provide funds for a personal secretary for the president. Polk paid out of his own pocket to have his nephew do the job.

4. Polk got Congress to declare war on Mexico, but it was not a universally popular decision. John Quincy Adams, still serving in the House of Representatives, called it a "most unrighteous war." A young congressman named Abraham Lincoln was not a fan of it either.

5. Because of his close association with Andrew Jackson, who was known as "Old Hickory," Polk was sometimes called "Young Hickory."

6. Polk declared at his inauguration, "I am the hardest working man in this country," which prompts me to declare, "James Polk might have had pride issues."

7. Martin Van Buren was elected president in 1836. He was defeated in 1840. In 1844 he was the early frontrunner to be the Democratic candidate again before Polk took the nomination from him.

8. Polk had hoped to be chosen as the vice presidential candidate in 1844. Getting the presidential nomination at the Democratic Convention was more than he bargained for.

9. Polk was the second president to promise to just serve one term. (Republican Rutherford B. Hayes was the third).

#12 Zachary Taylor

Political Party: Whig

Religious Affiliation: Episcopalian maybe

Home State when Elected: Louisiana

Time of Service: 3/4/1849-7/9/1850

Birth Date: November 24, 1784

Deceased: July 9, 1850

Zachary Taylor

1. He was the second president to die in office.

2. Taylor was born in Virginia, but while still a baby his family moved to Kentucky.

3. Taylor had some experience as a land surveyor before pursuing a career in the military.

4. Taylor was a hero in the Mexican War of 1846-1848.

5. He was nicknamed "Old Rough and Ready" by his men because he didn't worry so much about his appearance when he was out in the field, nor did he enjoy many personal amenities that weren't available to his troops.

6. While in the US Army, Taylor only appeared in uniform on very rare occasions. Such informality amused some of his men, but it was not a universally admired characteristic.

7. Years before Jefferson Davis was the President of the Confederate States of America, he became the son-in-law of Taylor. Taylor and his daughter both died many years before the Civil War.

8. Before getting elected president in 1848, Taylor had never voted in a presidential election.

9. Because Taylor was a war hero who had never voted, there was interest from both Democrats and Whigs in Taylor running for the presidency.

10. Taylor was even wooed by the small-time and controversial Native American Party (which was, ironically, made up entirely of white people).

11. Taylor died of natural causes (probably), but there was so much speculation that he had actually been poisoned that his corpse was dug up and examined in 1991. No evidence of poisoning was found (officially).

12. At slightly over 18 months, Taylor had the third shortest tenure of any American president.

#13 Milliard Fillmore

Political Party: Whig

Religious Affiliation: Unitarian

Home State when Sworn In: New York

Time of Service: 7/9/1850-3/4/1853

Birth Date: January 7, 1800

Deceased: March 8, 1874

Millard Fillmore

1. He's such an obscure figure that one book on American presidents was actually entitled *What's a Milliard Fillmore?*
2. Fillmore is such an obscure figure that when I revised this book, I did not bother adding any trivia about him.
3. He married his school teacher, which is not as creepy as it sounds. He was 18 when they met; she was 19.
4. Though he is a little-known figure today, Fillmore was actually pretty popular among his fellow politicians. One might think this is unremarkable, that all politicians who rise to the presidency must be charismatic people, but this is not the case. Richard Nixon and Jimmy Carter were neither very popular with their fellow politicians in Washington nor friendly with the majority of their staff members.
5. Fillmore was the last in a streak of four out of five Presidents who were Whigs. Of course two of the four were simply VP's finishing out the terms of their deceased bosses.

6. There was never another Whig President after Fillmore.

7. The first John Kennedy to serve in the Executive Branch worked for Fillmore. John P. Kennedy served as the secretary of the Navy in 1852-1853.

#14 Franklin Pierce

Political Party: Democratic

Religious Affiliation: Episcopalian

Home State when Elected: New Hampshire

Time of Service: 3/4/1853-3/4/1857

Birth Date: November 23, 1804

Deceased: October 8, 1869

Franklin Pierce

1. Pierce was considered quite good looking.

2. He was a military hero in the Mexican War.

3. He was nicknamed "Young Hickory of the Granite Hills." To which I say, "Enough already with the Hickory nicknames."

4. His Secretary of War (this position would later be re-titled "Secretary of Defense") was Jefferson Davis, the future President of the Confederate States of America.

5. Pierce is the only president who "affirmed" rather than "swore" his fidelity to the oath of office during his inauguration.

6. Pierce was the first president to have a Christmas tree at the White House.

#15 James Buchanan

Political Party: Democratic

Religious Affiliation: Presbyterian

Home State when Elected: Pennsylvania

Time of Service: 3/4/1857-3/4/1861

Birth Date: April 23, 1791

Deceased: June 1, 1868

James Buchanan

1. He is the only American president who never married.

2. Though unmarried, Buchanan was engaged for a while. At some point after the engagement was broken, Buchanan's ex died. He was not allowed to attend the funeral.

3. Many historians characterize Buchanan as a weak leader during a time of crisis (the secession of the southern states which prompted the Civil War). But I'm not sure what anyone could have done to keep the states together without going to war. Buchanan was already a lame duck when states began seceding, so it probably would have been bad for him to start a war and then leave office almost immediately.

4. Buchanan ran against the first Republican presidential candidate in American history, John Fremont, who went on to become a less-than-competent Civil War general for the Union.

5. Buchanan was the last secretary of state to become President of the United States. He had served in the Cabinet of James Polk.

#16 Abraham Lincoln

Political Party: Republican

Religious Affiliation: None

Home State when Elected: Illinois

Time of Service: 3/4/1861-4/15/1865

Birth Date: February 12, 1809

Deceased: April 15, 1865

Presidential Trivia 2.0

Abraham Lincoln

1. Lincoln was the first president to be born outside of the original 13 states.
2. Lincoln was the first of only two presidents to have served as a postmaster. This was actually great experience for a president to have because during this era, the president was the final authority over the United States Post Office.
3. Lincoln was the first Republican president, but before he was a Republican, he was a Whig.
4. Zachary Taylor's inauguration was significant to Lincoln for more than just being the last time a Whig was elected president. Lincoln also lost his hat at some point during the proceedings.
5. It was Lincoln who proclaimed we should celebrate Thanksgiving every year during November. This was in 1863, during the Civil War.
6. There had been state and local Thanksgiving celebrations in America dating back to the Puritans in 1621.

7. When Lincoln visited Union forces during the Civil War, he had something he liked to do for fun. He'd find tall soldiers, stand back to back with them, and have someone measure to see who was taller.

8. He had a very active sense of humor that was sometimes crude.

9. Though Lincoln talked about God and read his Bible a lot, he never joined a church.

10. Though he was never a church member, Lincoln did rent a pew in a Presbyterian Church late in life.

11. He is the only president to have had a patent. It was for a device that helped boats get through shallow river water.

12. Lincoln was only the second Republican to run for the presidency.

13. Today, Lincoln is considered one of our most popular and greatest presidents, but back then people weren't so sold on him. He won less than forty percent of the popular vote in 1860, and a lot of people thought he was going to lose in 1864 before he pulled it out.

14. Despite his struggles with popularity, Lincoln was the first president to be re-elected after Andrew Jackson.

#17 Andrew Johnson

Political Party: Republican

Religious Affiliation: None

Home State when Sworn In: Tennessee

Time of Service: 4/15/1865-3/4/1869

Birth Date: December 29, 1808

Deceased: July 31, 1875

Presidential Trivia 2.0

Andrew Johnson

1. The US has had plenty of men from poor families become president, but Johnson might have been the poorest.

2. Andrew Johnson was only 25 years old when he was elected Mayor of Greeneville, Tennessee. That's impressive, especially for a poor kid who came from out of state!

3. Johnson was a mayor, governor, Member of the House of Representatives, senator, vice president, and president. No other individual in American history has served in all those offices.

4. Johnson was the only member of Congress from a Confederate state who didn't resign from office at the outbreak of the Civil War.

5. Lincoln agreed to put him on the ticket because Lincoln felt it would show national unity (especially since Johnson was not just a southerner but a Democrat).

6. Though Tennessee was a Confederate state, East Tennessee where Johnson was from, favored the Union. There was even some talk of East Tennessee breaking off from the rest of the state, like the western counties of Virginia did when they formed West Virginia.

7. Because Johnson stayed with the Union, he was hated by most southern Democrats (at least for a while). Because he had been a lifelong Democrat and supported the interests of average southern whites as president, Johnson came to be despised by many Republicans. Thus, he was remarkably unpopular for a man who was elected to so many offices.

8. As stated above, Johnson liked the common (white) men in the South; he just resented the powerful plantation owners.

9. Lincoln's widow thought that Johnson was part of the conspiracy that killed the 16th president. She was probably wrong.

10. Johnson was the first president to be impeached. The Senate came one vote short of getting the 2/3's majority necessary to remove him from office.

11. During one particularly unfortunate speech, Johnson said he was the most unfairly vilified man since Jesus Christ. His (many) critics didn't really appreciate the comparison.

12. Speaking of Jesus, Johnson issued a Proclamation of Amnesty for Confederates on December 25, 1868. Merry Christmas, Rebels!

#18 Ulysses S. Grant

Political Party: Republican

Religious Affiliation: Methodist

Home State when Elected: Illinois

Time of Service: 3/4/1869-3/4/1877

Birth Date: April 27, 1822

Deceased: July 23, 1885

Presidential Trivia 2.0

Ulysses Grant

1. He was born with the first name "Hiram." The congressman who endorsed his efforts to get into West Point made a mistake with Grant's name, and Grant never corrected it.

2. Grant was unusually gifted at handling horses, even as a kid.

3. Grant's wife really disliked Mrs. Lincoln and forced Grant to get out of going to a play with the Lincolns called "Our American Cousin." It was on this occasion that Lincoln was assassinated. In other words, if Mary Todd Lincoln was easier to be around then Grant might have been assassinated years before ever becoming President.

4. He was the second Army officer to become a four-star general. George Washington was the first.

5. Though Grant's integrity is seldom questioned, his administration was one of the most corrupt in American history. He had dishonest men around him.

6. Grant got one thing right as president: It was on his watch that Christmas became a federal holiday.

7. Despite the corruption that tainted his administration, Grant wanted to be the first three-term President in American history. It shouldn't be surprising though; Grant's success in the Civil War was due to his refusal to quit in the face of adversity. He believed he could be a successful President if he just stuck with it. Republican Party leaders didn't agree and turned elsewhere.

8. His Civil War activities were so successful, and his presidential career so much the opposite, that when he wrote his memoirs he said nothing about his presidency at all.

#19 Rutherford B. Hayes

Political Party: Republican

Religious Affiliation: Methodist

Home State when Elected: Ohio

Time of Service: 3/4/1877-3/4/1881

Birth Date: October 4, 1822

Deceased: January 17, 1893

Presidential Trivia 2.0

Rutherford Hayes

1. He was a combat veteran of the Civil War.

2. Hayes also served as Ohio's governor.

3. His election victory was disputed because the counting of the votes in three states was compromised. Imagine if what happened in Florida in 2000 had occurred in two other states as well.

4. To calm the passions aroused by the disputed election, Rutherford pledged that he would not seek re-election in 1880.

5. Basically, though, the situation was resolved when southern Democrats were bribed with political considerations from northern Republicans. Nevertheless, critics called Rutherford "His Fraudulency."

6. His wife was such a supporter of the Temperance (anti-alcohol) movement, she was nicknamed "Lemonade Lucy." The President supported the movement also, but he was denied the privilege of getting a cool and alliterative nickname for his trouble.

#20 James Garfield

Political Party: Republican

Religious Affiliation: Disciples of Christ

Home State when Elected: Ohio

Time of Service: 3/4/1881-9/19/1881

Birth Date: November 19, 1831

Deceased: September 19, 1881

Presidential Trivia 2.0

James Garfield

1. He was our country's first left handed President.
2. Garfield is the only president to have also been an ordained minister.
3. He was also the first to have his mother attend his inauguration.
4. He was the third Civil War veteran to become president.
5. He was the second president to be assassinated.
6. Shot after about four months in office, he lingered for roughly three more months before passing away.
7. His six-and-a-half-month stint in office gives him the second-briefest presidency in American history.
8. Garfield didn't like having the responsibility of filling civil service jobs. He favored the creation of a test that could be used to slot candidates.
9. The man who killed the President was angry because his application for a civil service job had been denied. The application never actually made it to Garfield's

desk, so he bore no responsibility in causing his assassin's frustration.

#21 Chester A. Arthur

Political Party: Republican

Religious Affiliation: Episcopalian

Home State when Sworn In: New York

Time of Service: 9/19/1881-3/4/1885

Birth Date: October 5, 1830

Deceased: November 18, 1886

Presidential Trivia 2.0

Chester Arthur

1. Arthur was an advocate of civil service reform, which as mentioned earlier, would lead to hiring people based on their qualifications instead of the personal whimsy of the president.

2. The power of a president to fill civil service jobs had previously (starting with Andrew Jackson) been considered one of the main perks of the presidency. It frustrated the party bosses that Arthur signed civil service reform into legislation because Arthur's career was made by a political machine and the reform would weaken political machines. In other words, Arthur hurt the people who helped him in his rise to the top. But political machines weren't good for American politics. Thus, I guess you could say that Arthur was a good kind of hypocrite. How often does that happen?

3. Arthur didn't try hard to conceal the fact that the outcome of the 1880 election was influenced by political money buying votes in some areas. No

wonder the party bosses were mad when Arthur got all statesmanlike and wanted civil service reform.

4. He served in the Union Army during the Civil War.

5. Arthur was a widower in the White House. His wife actually died before he became vice president.

#22 Grover Cleveland

Political Party: Democratic

Religious Affiliation: Presbyterian

Home State when Elected: New York

Time of Service: 3/4/1885-3/4/1889

Birth Date: March 18, 1837

Deceased: June 24, 1908

Grover Cleveland

See the trivia under President #24.

#23 Benjamin Harrison

Political Party: Republican

Religious Affiliation: Presbyterian

Home State when Elected: Indiana

Time of Service: 3/4/1889-3/4/1893

Birth Date: August 20, 1833

Deceased: March 13, 1901

Benjamin Harrison

1. He was the grandson of William Henry Harrison. Given that Benjamin's father was the son of one President and the father of another; do you think Benjamin's dad might have struggled with feelings of not measuring up?

2. Actually, Benjamin's father, John Scott Harrison, did okay for himself politically, serving in the House of Representatives. And he died years before his son was elected president anyway.

3. Benjamin Harrison served in the Union Army in the Civil War.

4. He is considered the "Centennial President' because he was elected 100 years after George Washington.

5. Six states were admitted during Harrison's four years in office. No other president saw that many new states admitted in a single term.

#24 Grover Cleveland

Political Party: Democratic

Religious Affiliation: Presbyterian

Home State when Elected: New York

Time of Service: 3/4/1893-3/4/1897

Birth Date: March 18, 1837

Deceased: June 24, 1908

Presidential Trivia 2.0

Grover Cleveland

1. Cleveland was much older than his wife. He was a friend of her family and bought the first baby carriage her parents used for her. I can see where some people would find this kind of creepy. I know I did.
2. Cleveland and his wife didn't get married until he was already president.
3. He is the only president to serve terms in office that were not consecutive.
4. He is one of only three presidents to win the popular vote at least three times.
5. Despite winning so many popular votes, he was pretty unpopular by the end of his last term, thanks to a bad economy.
6. Cleveland was a conservative Democrat. He did not think the public should trust Congress with having a lot of money or power. Do you wonder what he would think today?

#25 William McKinley

Political Party: Republican

Religious Affiliation: Methodist

Home State when Elected: Ohio

Time of Service: 3/4/1897-9/14/1901

Birth Date: January 29, 1843

Deceased: September 14, 1901

William McKinley

1. He was president during the Spanish-American War.

2. He was the third president to be assassinated.

3. McKinley's political philosophy was not that different from Cleveland's—both men were conservative regarding the role of government. But a gold rush in Alaska helped the economy, and an easy military victory in the Spanish-American War made Americans proud. Because of these things, McKinley was pretty popular.

4. Because of Mrs. McKinley's poor physical and emotional health, she sat next to her husband during formal state dinners even though this went against tradition.

5. He served as governor of Ohio.

6. He was the fifth of five presidents who had fought for the Union in the Civil War.

#26 Theodore Roosevelt

Political Party: Republican

Religious Affiliation: Dutch Reformed

Home State when Sworn In: New York

Time of Service: 9/14/1901-3/4/1909

Birth Date: October 27, 1858

Deceased: January 6, 1919

Theodore Roosevelt

1. TR is the first President we know of who opened his Bible to a New Testament passage during his swearing-in ceremony. We are not sure which passage some of our earlier Presidents used.

2. Roosevelt quit his job as assistant secretary of the Navy, so he could join the Army and fight in the Spanish-American War.

3. Roosevelt was the first President to ride to his inauguration in an automobile. It was in 1905.

4. He was also the first sitting President to travel outside the country when he visited Latin America.

5. Another first? How about this one: He was the first US President to win a Nobel Peace Prize. It was for helping to negotiate the end of the Russo-Japanese War of 1904-1905.

6. Of all the vice presidents who took over after their President died in office, TR was the first to be elected in his own right after finishing out the term of the deceased.

7. Roosevelt previously had served as governor of New York.

8. Roosevelt was a prolific writer, authoring several books without the benefit of a ghost writer like so many modern politicians use.

9. His first wife and his mother, both of whom Roosevelt adored, died on the same day.

10. TR was so distraught about their deaths that he moved west, bought a ranch, and worked for a few years as a cowboy.

11. Roosevelt viewed the role of the president as that of a champion of the people. Such rhetoric is common nowadays, but it certainly was not the philosophy of Roosevelt's predecessors (except perhaps for Jackson, who saw himself as the champion of the average white men).

12. Roosevelt liked to push himself physically. As President, he power walked, hiked, learned judo, and loved to box. One day he was sparring with a young military officer who struck him and blinded the President in one eye. Roosevelt ended their session,

but he never let the officer know how badly the young man had hurt him.

13. At age 42, Roosevelt was the youngest man to ever become President of the United States.

14. TR was the first President to have an African American spend the night in the White House as a personal guest (as opposed to being a servant or slave).

#27 William Howard Taft

Political Party: Republican

Religious Affiliation: Unitarian

Home State when Elected: Ohio

Time of Service: 3/4/1909-3/4/1913

Birth Date: September 15, 1857

Deceased: March 8, 1930

Presidential Trivia 2.0

William Howard Taft

1. When he beat William Jennings Bryan in the 1908 election. It was the third time Bryan had lost to a man named William. The first two times it was William McKinley.

2. Taft might be most well-known for being so large (roughly 350 lbs.) that he got stuck in the White House bath tub.

3. Taft was reluctant to run for the presidency in 1908 and really didn't enjoy the job. Yet when his close friend Theodore Roosevelt tried to re-take the position, Taft fought him for it. This was quite the bump in the road for the friendship.

4. In the Election of 1912 Taft suffered the humiliation of finishing third in the popular vote. No other President in American history has had to endure such a distinction.

5. Parenthetically, Taft later regained his warm feelings for his friend. It kind of reminds me of the relationship between John Adams and Thomas Jefferson.

6.   Taft later became Chief Justice of the Supreme Court.

Presidential Trivia 2.0

#28 Woodrow Wilson

Political Party: Democratic

Religious Affiliation: Presbyterian

Home State when Elected: New Jersey

Time of Service: 3/4/1913-3/4/1921

Birth Date: December 28, 1856

Deceased: February 3, 1924

Woodrow Wilson

1. He once famously said, "It would be the irony of fate if my administration had to deal chiefly with foreign affairs." It turned out to be an ironic quotation— Wilson was president during World War One.

2. Wilson was president when the United States implemented the federal income tax via the 16th Amendment. Um, thanks, Mr. President.

3. Though he was elected twice, Wilson never won a majority of the popular vote. Both times he simply won a plurality. It didn't really matter though because he won a majority of the electoral votes both times.

4. Wilson was the governor of New Jersey.

5. He also served as the president of Princeton.

6. Despite Wilson's rise to academic prominence, he struggled as a young student. By the end of what would be considered elementary school today, Wilson could barely read, demonstrating that sometimes in life it's not where you start, but where you finish, that matters.

7. Wilson won a Nobel Peace Prize for his efforts during and after World War One.

8. Though he was a progressive (liberal) Democrat, Wilson would be an awkward fit today for either political party. He openly disdained African Americans, and his views on immigrants were also clearly racist.

#29 Warren Harding

Political Party: Republican

Religious Affiliation: Baptist

Home State when Elected: Ohio

Time of Service: 3/4/1921-8/2/1923

Birth Date: November 2, 1865

Deceased: August 2, 1923

Warren Harding

1. Harding is considered to have had one of the most corrupt administrations in American history.
2. His secretary of the interior, Albert Fall, was the first Cabinet official in American history to go to prison.
3. Lasting less than a month longer than Zachary Taylor, Harding has the fourth shortest term in office among all the presidents.
4. Officially, Harding died of a heart attack, but some have speculated that he did not die of natural causes. Their reasoning is that his demise, self-inflicted or otherwise, was prompted by the increasing exposure of the corruption in his administration.
5. Some people believe that Harding became a member of the Ku Klux Klan while President, but there are other historians who are quite skeptical of this.
6. Harding was the one who nominated former President Taft for the Supreme Court.

#30 Calvin Coolidge

Political Party: Republican

Religious Affiliation: Congregationalist

Home State when Sworn In: Massachusetts

Time of Service: 8/2/1933-3/4/1929

Birth Date: July 4, 1872

Deceased: January 5, 1933

Calvin Coolidge

1. Coolidge is the only President we know of who turned his Bible open to one of the Gospels during his swearing in ceremony. He chose John 1:1.
2. Speaking of religion, Coolidge was a Congregationalist, which was the denomination of the Puritans.
3. He was the last president to visit Cuba before Barack Obama traveled there in 2016.
4. Coolidge was famous for being sparse with words—an unusual trait for a man who spent his career in politics.
5. He was one of only four VP's to take over for a deceased president then get elected to serve a full term as president in the next election.
6. Three American Presidents have died on July 4; Coolidge is our only president to be born on that day.
7. Coolidge was a governor of Massachusetts.

#31 Herbert Hoover

Political Party: Republican

Religious Affiliation: Society of Friends (Quaker)

Home State when Elected: California

Time of Service: 3/4/1929-3/4/1933

Birth Date: August 10, 1874

Deceased: October 20, 1964

Presidential Trivia 2.0

Herbert Hoover

1. Hoover's vice president, Charles Curtis, was partially Native American. This was something the campaign emphasized in 1928.
2. Hoover and his wife, Lou, could speak Mandarin (Chinese), which came in handy when they wanted to speak confidentially in the presence of others.
3. Hoover was one of only two Quakers two be president. Richard Nixon was the other.
4. He is the only US president was an engineer.
5. Hoover is only the second left handed President. There were several more after him.
6. Hoover served in the Cabinet as the Secretary of Commerce for Warren Harding and Calvin Coolidge.
7. Hoover was given honorary citizenship in Belgium for his work in providing food for that country during and after World War One. He also helped them after World War Two.
8. He was the first president to have a telephone on his office desk. Texting came much later.

#32 Franklin Roosevelt

Political Party: Democratic

Religious Affiliation: Episcopalian

Home State when Elected: New York

Time of Service: 3/4/1933-4/12/1945

Birth Date: January 30, 1882

Deceased: April 12, 1945

Franklin Roosevelt

1. Roosevelt was the first candidate to accept his party's convention nomination in person. Earlier candidates tried to project the image of the reluctant, unambitious hero, but FDR wanted to project the image of someone who was ready to get to work.

2. FDR signed into law the current method of determining when Americans celebrate Thanksgiving. This federal holiday is on the fourth Thursday in November.

3. Roosevelt appointed the first female Cabinet member, Frances Perkins, as secretary of labor.

4. Roosevelt is the only American president to win four presidential elections. His rationale for serving so many times was that with the Great Depression and World War Two both going on, it was no time to hand things over to a rookie.

5. FDR is the only President to have three vice presidents (but not at the same time. That would have been wrong).

6. Except for being in a different political party, FDR patterned his career after that of his famous, distant cousin, Theodore Roosevelt. Both were governors of New York and assistant secretaries of the Navy. TR served as vice president, and FDR ran as a VP candidate in the Election of 1920.

7. FDR also tried to project an image of physicality since that was a part of TR's persona. It was tough for FDR, though, since his legs were crippled by polio. The media helped hide the extent of his infirmity. Cultivating the media was another strategy that FDR borrowed from TR.

8. FDR was the first president to engage in illegal wiretapping of suspected traitors (it was World War Two) and political enemies. He was certainly not the last [Richard Nixon comes to mind (among others)].

#33 Harry S Truman

Political Party: Democratic

Religious Affiliation: Baptist

Home State when Sworn In: Missouri

Time of Service: 4/12/1945-1/20/1953

Birth Date: May 8, 1884

Deceased: December 26, 1972

Presidential Trivia 2.0

Harry S Truman

1. Truman only has an "S," not a middle name.

2. He was the second of only two US presidents who served as a postmaster earlier in life. It might not be as impressive as leading us to victory in World War Two, but it did seem appropriate for inclusion in a book of presidential trivia.

3. Famed evangelist Billy Graham met with and provided spiritual counsel to all the Presidents of the mid to late 20th Century. Harry Truman was the first.

4. Truman is the only man to be President during two different wars. They were World War Two and the Korean War. (George W. Bush and Barack Obama might argue that they fought multiple wars, in Iraq and Afghanistan, but both of these locations were part of the same conflict—the War on Terror.)

5. Truman's popularity when he left office was roughly as low as that of Richard Nixon and George W. Bush.

6. Truman fought in World War One.

7. It was during Truman's administration that the United States went from having a Secretary of War to a Secretary of Defense.

#34 Dwight Eisenhower

Political Party: Republican

Religious Affiliation: Presbyterian

Home State when Elected: New York

Time of Service: 1/20/1953-1/20/1961

Birth Date: October 14, 1890

Deceased: March 28, 1969

Dwight Eisenhower

1. Eisenhower (Ike) was so popular that he could have run for either party in the 1952 election.

2. He was so popular that Harry Truman, the sitting President of the United States, offered to be Ike's VP, if Eisenhower wanted to run as a Democrat. Of course, Truman was so unpopular at that point, the offer wasn't that enticing. But it is impressive that Ike's stature elicited it.

3. Ike's popularity was such that Democrats decided the best way to defeat him in 1952 was to raise questions about the character of his young running mate, Richard Nixon. It obviously didn't work, but it did impact the relationship between the two Republicans. Nixon felt Ike should have been quicker to show his support. But Eisenhower did not know Nixon, and Ike was being encouraged to not take a chance on him, so Nixon actually got more support than he realized.

4. Ike was so beloved because he led American forces to victory in the European Theater during World War Two.

5. Before running for the presidency, Ike had never voted in a presidential election. This was not a result of apathy. As an Army officer, Ike wanted to be able to serve in good conscience whichever political party ruled the White House.

6. Ike is responsible for our modern interstate highway system.

#35 John F. Kennedy

Political Party: Democratic

Religious Affiliation: Catholic

Home State when Elected: Massachusetts

Time of Service: 1/20/1961-11/22/1963

Birth Date: May 29, 1917

Deceased: November 22, 1963

John Kennedy

1. Kennedy was the first president to later have a brother make a run for the White House. Robert Kennedy was a serious candidate for the Democratic nomination in the 1968 Election before being assassinated by a Palestinian sympathizer.

2. Some rivals feared a "Kennedy Dynasty," which would have featured John, Robert, and another brother—Edward. Edward Kennedy went on to become a longtime senator.

3. Before becoming president, John Kennedy wrote *Profiles in Courage*, which detailed the circumstances of several politicians who took unpopular, career-threatening stands simply because they believed it was the right thing to do.

4. Kennedy has been our only Catholic president.

5. Kennedy became a war hero because of his exploits in the Pacific Theater during World War Two.

6. Eisenhower had won a significant percentage of the African American vote in 1952 and 1956. Kennedy,

however, captured a strong majority of the African American vote in 1960, and the Democratic Party has built on that advantage ever sense.

7. At the age of 43, Kennedy was the youngest man elected president. Teddy Roosevelt was younger than Kennedy when Roosevelt became president, but Roosevelt was filling in for the deceased McKinley.

8. Kennedy died on the same date as the famous British Christian writer CS Lewis.

9. Kennedy was the first American president born in the 20th Century.

Presidential Trivia 2.0

#36 Lyndon B. Johnson

Political Party: Democratic

Religious Affiliation: Disciples of Christ

Home State when Sworn In: Texas

Time of Service: 11/22/1963-1/20/1969

Birth Date: August 27, 1908

Deceased: January 22, 1973

Lyndon Johnson

1. Johnson was so unpopular because of the Vietnam War and his support of civil rights reform that he lost the first Democratic primary in the 1968 election. He responded by saying that he needed to focus on winning the war, so he would not run for re-election.

2. His fall in stature is all the more remarkable when one considers that he won by a landslide in 1964.

3. Johnson chose the first African American Cabinet officer. It was Robert Weaver, who was the secretary of the Housing and Urban Development.

4. Johnson wanted to be as popular as Franklin Roosevelt and even more so than John Kennedy.

5. Because of his focus on FDR, Johnson wanted to be known by his initials—LBJ.

6. Before taking over after Kennedy's assassination, Johnson was the first VP with an office in the White House.

7. LBJ was the last of the four VP's who got sworn in when the President died in office then got elected to serve a full term as President during the next election.

8. Johnson had a practice of engaging aides in conversation then leading them to the bathroom. Johnson would continue his conversation as he, um, took full advantage of the facilities. Demonstrating his personal authority and control like that was important to him. And it was rather gross.

#37 Richard M. Nixon

Political Party: Republican

Religious Affiliation: Society of Friends (Quaker)

Home State when Elected: New York

Time of Service: 1/20/1969-8/9/1974

Birth Date: January 9, 1913

Deceased: April 22, 1994

Richard Nixon

1. Nixon grew up in California, but he settled in New York in the 1960s before his run for the presidency in 1968.

2. Nixon was one of our best prepared presidents. As a young man he served in a low-ranking office in the Executive Branch. After World War Two, he was a member of the House of Representatives then a senator then vice president under Dwight Eisenhower.

3. As a Quaker, Nixon could have avoided military service in World War Two, but he served anyway— years before a political career was a realistic option— and spent time in the War in the Pacific.

4. Nixon was so taken with his future wife, Pat, that when she was dating other men, he would drive her to meet her dates, wait around, then bring her back home. A tale of enduring love, or kind of creepy? You decide.

5. He was a pretty fair piano player.

6. His political career was almost derailed years before Watergate. As Eisenhower's running mate in the 1952

election, Nixon was accused of having a secret slush fund. Nixon countered the charges by getting on TV and discussing his personal finances with the public. It was known as "the Checkers Speech" and it won (the Republican) public over to him.

7. Nixon ran for governor of California in 1962 and lost. He had already lost a bid for the presidency in 1960. These two defeats led many to believe that his career in politics was over.

8. Nixon helped end the military draft in America.

9. The US had no formal relations with China from the time of the Communist takeover in 1949 until after Nixon became president. Perhaps the main thing that helped Nixon sell the American people on the idea of good relations with China, despite the reality that we were in a Cold War against communism, was the fact that Nixon had been such a virulent anti-Communist. If he could trust them, so could we.

10. When Nixon resigned over the Watergate Scandal, he did not admit wrongdoing. He said it was because he had lost his ability to govern (since it was obvious

Congress didn't support him—they were preparing to impeach him then throw him out).

11. Unlike most historians, I believe Nixon knew about the Watergate break-ins ahead of time. If you want to know why, read my book, *Nixon and His Men: The Road through Watergate*, if you can find a copy, which is hard because it is out of print.

12. You'll note above that I wrote "break-ins." There were actually two of them in the Watergate building.

#38 Gerald R. Ford

Political Party: Republican

Religious Affiliation: Episcopalian

Home State when Elected: Michigan

Time of Service: 8/9/1974-1/20/1977

Birth Date: July 14, 1913

Deceased: December 26, 2006

Presidential Trivia 2.0

Gerald Ford

1. He was born with the name "Leslie King Jr."

2. Ford was an avid golfer.

3. Ford was the only man to serve as president who was never elected to national office (not as VP or president).

4. Ford became vice president when Nixon's first VP, Spiro Agnew, had to resign because of corruption (unrelated to Watergate).

5. Ford took over the White House when Nixon resigned.

6. Because of his political background, Ford never dreamed of being President; his goal was to be Speaker of the House.

7. Irony alert: Ford was considered a klutz (and famously portrayed that way in "Saturday Night Live" skits) because he slipped while walking down an icy ramp coming off an airplane. Actually, Ford wasn't clumsy at all; he was an All American football player who had the opportunity to play in the NFL.

8. Ford turned down a career in the NFL because there was little money or security there then. Instead he became a college assistant coach because that paid his way through law school.

9. Despite the fact that Ronald Reagan challenged Ford's candidacy in 1976, there was some serious talk of making Ford the running mate of Reagan in the 1980 election. A former president climbing back on board as VP? Truman had been open to it earlier, but it has still never happened in American history.

#39 James E. Carter

Political Party: Democratic

Religious Affiliation: Baptist

Home State when Elected: Georgia

Time of Service: 1/20/1977-1/20/1981

Birth Date: October 1, 1924

Jimmy Carter

1. He was the first president to be born in a hospital.

2. He was an avid tennis player.

3. He served as governor of Georgia.

4. Carter was the first president since Chester Arthur to push civil service reform through Congress.

5. He was the first president since Herbert Hoover to get elected to a first term but voted out of a second term.

6. Carter is known for boycotting the 1980 Olympics in response to the Soviet invasion of Afghanistan. The boycott angered many Americans who were increasingly frustrated by the Carter administration, but the invasion didn't turn out so well for the Soviets either, so there's that.

7. He helped broker the first peace treaty between Israel and a Middle Eastern country (Egypt).

8. Surprisingly for someone with such a pleasant smile, Carter was rather cold with people he didn't know, and he was not very affirming with his aides. It didn't help that he ran as an outsider who complained about

Washington's ways because that approach alienated potential allies once he got there.

9. Carter raised eyebrows by having his wife, Rosalyn, attend Cabinet meetings. His rationale was that he was going to ask her for advice anyway, so it made since that she should have an informed opinion on things. Americans were troubled that she wasn't voted in by the American people or formally approved by the Senate. Of course, it was also the 1970s, and some people were just bothered by it because she was a woman.

10. Carter was quite outspoken about his Christian faith, yet many evangelical Christians turned to Ronald Reagan in the 1980 election. Reagan was a Christian, too, but he did not talk about his faith as easily as Carter.

11. In 2002, Carter won a Nobel Peace Prize.

#40 Ronald W. Reagan

Political Party: Republican

Religious Affiliation: Presbyterian

Home State when Elected: California

Time of Service: 1/20/1981-1/20/1989

Birth Date: February 6, 1911

Deceased: June 5, 2004

Presidential Trivia 2.0

Ronald Reagan

1. After Inauguration Day was moved to January, Reagan had the warmest inauguration recorded (as of 2016). It was 55 degrees in 1981.
2. Lest one blame that on global warming, Reagan's next inauguration was the coldest at 7 degrees in 1985.
3. Martin Luther King Day became a national holiday during Reagan's presidency.
4. Reagan was a rather popular television and movie personality.
5. He also worked as a sports broadcaster on the radio.
6. He was a two-term governor of California.
7. He first got involved in politics when he was actor. He ran for president of the Screen Actors Guild because he was concerned about a communist takeover of the SAG and Hollywood in general. Seriously.
8. Reagan had been a Democrat who voted for Franklin Roosevelt.
9. When Reagan ran for re-election in 1984, he won 49 states. Reagan's opponent, Walter Mondale, won

Minnesota and the District of Columbia. Only three presidential elections were more lopsided than this (Washington twice and Monroe's re-election), and those men ran unopposed. Ouch, Mondale.

10. Despite tough talk, and occasionally tough actions, on foreign policy, Reagan's legacy was tarnished by the Iran-Contra Scandal, which included an indirect accommodation of Middle Eastern terrorists.

11. Reagan's Star Wars Initiative, a plan to intercept nuclear missiles before they could strike the United States, was mocked by critics as ridiculously expensive and technologically impossible. But it did make the Soviets feel compelled to pour money into their own defense program. Since the Soviets couldn't afford this, it helped unravel their government and end the Cold War.

Presidential Trivia 2.0

#41 George H. W. Bush

Political Party: Republican

Religious Affiliation: Episcopalian

Home State when Elected: Texas

Time of Service: 1/20/1989-1/20/1993

Birth Date: June 12, 1924

126

George H. W. Bush

1. The elder Bush and his son make up only the second father-son presidential duo.

2. George Bush played baseball for Yale.

3. Several future Presidents served in the Pacific Theater during World War Two, but Bush, like John Kennedy, was legitimately a war hero there. Bush served as a pilot and got shot down by the Japanese.

4. Bush served as Director of the CIA.

5. Bush is remembered for bragging during the 1988 campaign that when Congress pressured him to agree to raise taxes, he would say, "Read my lips: No new taxes!" He got elected President but ended up agreeing to the biggest tax increase in American history. It didn't win him the love of liberals, but it made some conservatives hate him.

6. His approval rating at one point was almost 90%, but he failed in his bid for re-election. This was at least partially because of an economic recession.

7. In 2016, he and his wife Barbara celebrated their 71st wedding anniversary, giving them the longest marriage of any presidential couple in American history.

#42 William J. Clinton

Political Party: Democratic

Religious Affiliation: Southern Baptist

Home State when Elected: Arkansas

Time of Service: 1/20/1993-1/20/2001

Birth Date: August 19, 1946

Presidential Trivia 2.0

Bill Clinton

1. Clinton served as a member of the Electoral College in 2016 and cast a vote for his wife, Hillary.
2. As of 2016, Clinton is the only president to have his wife run for the presidency, which she did in 2008 and 2016.
3. He's also the only one to have a wife elected to the US Senate and named secretary of state.
4. Clinton was born with the name "Billy Blythe." His father died in a car wreck, and Clinton later took the name of his stepfather.
5. He was an avid golfer and jogger.
6. Clinton won the presidency twice while garnering just a plurality of the popular vote.
7. Part of the difficulty for Clinton in winning a popular vote majority was the relatively strong third party candidacy of billionaire businessman Ross Perot.
8. Clinton was just the second US President to be impeached, though the Senate fell well below the 2/3's majority necessary to remove him from office.

9. Despite Clinton's lack of a majority of the popular vote and his impeachment, he left office with high job approval ratings.

10. Though he bristled at the comparison, Clinton bore several similarities to Jimmy Carter. Both were moderate Democrats who served as governors from southern states. Both ran as outsiders from the Washington establishment and pledged to clean up the corruption there.

11. Clinton changed the way candidates compete when he made an appearance during the 1992 campaign on "The Arsenio Hall Show" (a popular late night program) and performed on the saxophone.

12. As a teenager, Clinton met John Kennedy and shook his hand. Clinton decided then that he wanted to be like Kennedy. Impressively, Clinton accomplished his goal and became president. Unimpressively, he emulated his predecessor's poor sexual morals and lack of respect for marital vows.

13. Clinton was the first Democratic president since Franklin Roosevelt to serve two full terms.

#43 George W. Bush

Political Party: Republican

Religious Affiliation: Methodist

Home State when Elected: Texas

Time of Service: 1/20/2001-1/20/2009

Birth Date: July 6, 1946

George W. Bush

1. In 1989 Bush bought a minority share of the ownership of Major League baseball's Texas Rangers.

2. Bush later served as a popular two-term governor of Texas.

3. Though Bush's intelligence was questioned by his political enemies, he is the only president in American history to earn degrees from both Harvard and Yale.

4. He is only the second president, and first Republican, to have a brother later run for the presidency. Jeb Bush unsuccessfully sought the Republican nomination in 2016.

5. In the 2000 election Bush received fewer popular votes than Al Gore, but Bush received more electoral votes. In 2004, Bush won re-election and a majority of the popular vote.

6. The 2000 election is remembered for the dispute over the Florida voting results. As both sides fought for the victory there, the Democrat-dominated Florida Supreme Court tended to favor Gore in its rulings, and

the Republican-dominated US Supreme Court eventually handed Bush the victory.

7. When Bush was elected the second time, it was the first time in American history that a two-term president from one party, Bill Clinton, was followed by a two-term president from the opposition party.

8. When Bush won a majority of the popular vote in 2004, it was the first such occurrence since his father won a popular majority in 1988.

#44 Barack H. Obama

Political Party: Democratic

Religious Affiliation: Church of Christ

Home State when Elected: Illinois

Time of Service: 1/20/2009-1/20/2017

Birth Date: August 4, 1961

Presidential Trivia 2.0

Barack Obama

1. America had not had a two-term president from one party succeeded by a two-termer from the other party until Clinton and the second Bush. The re-election of Obama in 2012 continued the trend.

2. He won two Grammys for reading his books on CD.

3. Obama was such a basketball fan that he filled out an NCAA Tournament bracket every March.

4. Obama is America's first mixed race President—his mother was white, his father was Kenyan.

5. We have had some charismatic Presidents recently, like Bill Clinton and Ronald Reagan, but apparently, Obama is in a class by himself. A white, male reporter for NBC shared that covering Obama made him weak in the knees. A white, male TV personality on MSNBC said hearing Obama speak gave him a tingle in his leg. One assumes these men did not feel similar sensations when covering Obama's Republican opponent, John McCain.

6. A surprising number of Americans believed circa 2010 that Obama was secretly a Muslim. I say if people all over the country think they know such a thing then it is one poorly kept secret. Obama has consistently said that he became a Christian back in the 1980s.

7. Obama is the first American President to be born after the Korean War.

8. In 2009 he won the Nobel Peace Prize.

9. He is only the eighth left handed President in American history.

#45 Donald Trump

Political Party: Republican

Religious Affiliation: None

Home State when Elected: New York

Time of Service: 1/20/2017-?

Birth Date: June 14, 1946

Donald Trump

1. Trump is the first president who did not become famous through politics or the military. He originally became a national figure as a business tycoon.

2. He raised his profile by becoming a television star, a distinction among presidents that he shares with Ronald Reagan, but Regan, of course, was also a governor before becoming president.

3. Trump is only the second divorced president in American history; yet another commonality he shares with Reagan.

4. Trump is the only president to be divorced twice and married three times.

5. His third wife, Melania, was born in the former country of Yugoslavia.

6. Trump's presidential victory, coupled with his lack of political experience, is all the more ironic considering the experience of his

139

opponent. Hillary Clinton was a secretary of state, United States senator, lawyer, the First Lady of the United States, and the First Lady of Arkansas. Despite all of that, plus winning the popular vote, Mrs. Clinton was unable to get the majority of the Electoral College voters.

7. Another irony alert: After the 2016 Election popular vote was counted, Democrats launched an unprecedented campaign to get some of the Electoral College members to "vote their conscience." Ultimately some Electors got replaced for refusing to vote for their party's choice, but seven voters cast rogue votes. Two Republicans voted for other Republicans besides Trump. Five Democrat Electors voted against Clinton.

8. Guests at Trump's third wedding included Bill and Hillary Clinton. I assume they brought a gift. I wonder if they wish they could take it back.

9. Kellyanne Conway, who ran Trump's campaign, is the first woman to ever successfully run a presidential campaign. Who would have thought that Trump would be a pioneer in creating opportunities for women?

About the Author

Timothy D. Holder is the author of over a dozen books, including *Presidential Character*, which looks at the first six presidents and their views on faith, race, and leadership.

Dr. Holder is a Professor of History at Walters State Community College in Tennessee. He holds a Ph. D. and MA in History from the University of Kentucky, a MAAT in Applied Theology from Carson-Newman University, and a BA with majors in Bible and Education from Asbury University.

Holder is also a public speaker who enjoys talking about the presidents and creative writing. And he's the author of the *Logan Franklin Chronicles*, a military sci-fi ebook series.

Website address: www.tdhcommunications.com.

CPSIA information can be obtained
at www.ICGtesting.com
Printed in the USA
LVHW081311190220
647479LV00017B/619

9 781541 356511